Soundings

Poems and Drawings by
Cilla McQueen

Published by University of Otago Press
PO Box 56/56 Union Street West, Dunedin, New Zealand
Fax: 64 3 479 8385; email: university.press@otago.ac.nz

First published 2002
Copyright © Cilla McQueen 2002
ISBN 1 877276 38 3

Printed by
Printlink Ltd, Wellington

Acknowledgements
A grant from Creative New Zealand assisted with the writing of this book.
Some of these poems have been published in *Landfall* and *New Zealand Books*.
The poem 'Fuse' was commissioned for the Parihaka exhibition and book jointly
produced by the City Gallery, Wellington, and the Parihaka Pa Trustees.
The quote in 'Tourists (ii)' is from Bill Manhire talking about Antarctica
on National Radio's Nine to Noon poetry programme.

Published with the assistance of
Creative New Zealand

Poems

Drawings

To my mother
and to Stewart Whaitiri

Riddles (i)

1
my bone
takes my flesh
to your lips

2
my wings
sweep earth
from the earth

3
you walk
on my head –
my neck, your ankle

4
my jaws
hold down
the roof

5
dreaming
I cover you
like cloud

6
I burn,
illuminate your
feast of me

Riddles (ii)

'No part of the gannet was ever wasted.'

Make a spoon of my breastbone
and of my wings a feather broom.

My head makes a soft shoe laced at the throat,
my beak a stout peg, to anchor the thatch.

Featherdown is your bed in the storm.
I give strength to your body

and brightness to your eyes –
your lamp is my clear oil flame.

Ruapuke Island

Te Motu Kaika Kuri

Daughter

Remember pipit, petrel, whimbrel,
gannet, curlew, swallow

wheeling above the green apron,
the ruined eaves, Conachair's shadow;

that the Stone of Knowledge
gives you second sight,

the clear, light water of a certain well
the power to change the wind.

Ancient

i

'Conceive, if you can, a sort of green bosom, with steep green mountains, and on one side with a fine bay opening into rocky scenery … in the centre several green tufts of grassy sod, upon heaps of loose stones – these we at last discovered to be the houses, twenty-six in number … This is the town or city of Hirta, or St Kilda. It contains 100 inhabitants … (Lord Brougham, 1799)

ii

The storm takes no hold
of a corbelled beehive,
but skims the turf roof
of the old black house.

Quiet burns within
on the smooth earth floor,
peat fire in the hearth
in a circle of stone.

Tourists (i)

At the least, the tourist brings
the boat-cold.

We have little immunity
from the world's disease.

Curiosities, we climb the cliffs
for their amusement,

accept their coins
and give them gannets' eggs,

while the shadows of our ancestors
bloom at our heels along the cliffs

that take our breath away,
as the tourist takes away our marrow.

Resistance

Time once was measured by the sun,
the shadows cast by rocks, the flight of birds
that marked the seasons changing.
Hours fell like feathers.

When the minister's timepiece
effaced the natural calendar,
time was measured by attendance at the church;

the rhythms of old that made the people dance all day
replaced by the thump of his fist on the pulpit,
hammering the Gaelic out of them – English
carried the burden of brimstone and penitence.

But all through the birding and plucking,
the spinning and weaving and making,
the old songs still trickled like laughter.

St Kilda, 1799

A sail on the horizon! We man our boat
as our wives prepare the households

for flight across the island
to the safety of the Glen.

Six men and our minister row out to the ship.
The English have opened their armschest,

fearing our sheepskin dress,
our wild appearance –

yet we are gentle as chicks,
without guile but for survival.

Their manners are very stiff,
their English speech strange-sounding –

'sark-ag-ag-ag-ag' on a rising, anxious note,
resembling the cackling of the fulmar.

A Fright, 1838

When the steamship *Vulcan* appeared in the Bay
we ran to the minister – a ship on fire

with no sails left, smoke issuing from it!
Then a troop of soldiers disembarked

and marched up the village street
with trumpet and drum!

Trumpet and drum resounded from the crags
as we fled behind our mountain.

To our stout minister alone the troop proclaimed
the succession of Queen Victoria, and steamed away.

A Cleit

To make a cleit
to store the grain

and dry salt birds
and winter peat,

build small flat boulders
to a dome

with holes between
to let through wind,

and turf on top
to keep out rain.

Savage

'A total want of curiosity, a stupid gaze of wonder, an excessive eagerness for spirits
and tobacco, a laziness only to be conquered by the hope of the above mentioned
cordials, and a beastly degree of filth, the natural consequence of this, render the
St Kildan character truly savage.' (Lord Brougham, 1799)

Without question we accept the deities.
Nothing much is lost; when our father's house falls down
we use his stones to build another.
What stays fallen, turf covers.

When a man falls, a rib is torn from us.
When John went over Oiseval like a starfish, the sea had him.

Conachair is the mountain.
From the heights of our cloudmaker a sail on the horizon
might be, or not, a fleck of light.

We trust in God and in our fellow man.
Visitors are another matter.

Once two ruffians came ashore and set fire to the church
and entire congregation,
and only the Little Old Woman of the Red Fell was saved,
who was hiding in the crags.

We descend from the mountain with caution
when visitors come ashore.

Our life by the natural calendar might be construed as laziness
by the visitor who brings his timepiece with him,
to amaze us with its ticking cogs.

In our dark and simple land
we follow the cliff paths of our ancestors,
lamenting our frailty, killing birds with precision.

One of us was struck with wonder, on visiting Glasgow,
at horses that towed small wheeled houses behind them
on streets of stones so small and regular they might be hewn,
except no man could have the patience, or stupidity.

There is a medicinal whisky bottle
behind the door-post, for emergencies.
As for tobacco, we can't get enough.
It reminds us of the smouldering peat.

Eyes gleam in the firelight while the tempest rages.
Oh the laziness and filth of this mortal life!
Only the hope of the cordials of heaven moves us.

Perhaps we are confusing overseas with heaven.
Gillies was the catalyst – off to California, Australia,
New Zealand, home again but couldn't settle, ended up in Canada.

It was the filth he couldn't settle back to –
nor could his foreign wife, who called us savages.
We sleep with the animals. The floor is beaten dung.
It piles up in the winter; we dig it out in spring.

Eyes gleam in the firelight.
We might have a medicinal whisky while the tempest rages
and the wind beams through cracks in the stones –

a little moss will make us snug,
for whoever sleeps the night long on the slopes of Conachair
awakes a poet in the morning.

Pastoral

Coming south, the traffic lessened
until at Tuturau there was nothing
but silent landscape, humming river.

Auckland was all cars.
I felt like that visitor to Glasgow

who saw with amazement
the mechanism of the coach-wheel
and its running about,
exclaimed at the long-heeled women,

found oak trees indescribable
on his return to St Kilda,
where the Least Willow grows
barely two inches tall.

The High Church seemed to him
a most prodigious hand-made rock,

but when the great bells rang
he clapped his hands to his ears in terror –
he thought they rent the fabric of the world.

Early Settlers

The tall sequoia dwarfs the obelisk
in the other corner of the park

from which I gently peel away
the children on the swings,
removing layers until I find myself
running across the uneven green to primary school.

When the park was made in 1879
the Early Settlers' graves were swept
into a low mound, a small Cleopatra's Needle
placed on top.

In 1869, during the Gold Rush, a regiment
brought in for the control of undesirables
camped in the overgrown graveyard

where in 1865 scientists prepared
remarkable exhibits for Dunedin's Exhibition

in temporary buildings erected in 1861
to house a lunatic asylum
(later removed to Seacliff).

In 1858 the York Place Cemetery was closed.
Somebody knelt beside a rainy grave
and pressed a sequoia seed into the earth.

Fuse

The road winds back in time
as we drive down the Otago Peninsula
to Te Rauone. It is a visit,
a kind of unveiling – in my mind
the meeting house at Otakou,
Weller's rock, the fishing wharf,
and around the corner a wooden house
with an orange roof and a pohutukawa tree.

A long stone wall runs beside the road
from the head of the harbour
all the way along the peninsula northwards,
a blue-black drystone wall
built by the Maori prisoners from Parihaka.
This wall runs back in time –
in one of these small bays
you might see soldiers at ease under a tree
toss crumbs to seagulls
while they watch the Taranaki men break rock.

Fire springs from the curved steel pick;
anger drives deep inside the lizard wall
that twists through torn fields of their sleep
in stone cells cut in the cliff
where clay walls sweat like dying men.
The scarred moon blesses the hands of whanau
that twine at the bars like roots.
Te Whiti's words, white feathers, fill the darkness.
A candle, a murmur of prayer.
At night the iron-barred window sings.

The lizard flickers its tongue
as we pass the fishing wharf, the small boats,
and round the corner – there is Te Rauone beach,

the sandhills, seagrass, Taiaroa Head beyond,
the seabirds, the channel, Aramoana –
only there is no house
and in the ground no trace of ash,
just soft green lupins,
growing in clean sand,
red stars on the pohutukawa.

Loss of possessions is a kind of freedom;
loss of the land is exile.
The pickaxes strike fire.
The wall runs back towards the city,
a fuse slow-burning through the generations
ready to flare; past time nearly visible
behind the surface of this sunny day,
the harbour sparkling – on the car radio, news
of an unarmed Maori man
shot dead by the police last night, in Waitara.

(May, 2000)

Eating the News

Like Cheezels the News –
from behind irascible mountains
the newly dead appear.

I go out to talk to the silver beet
in the vegetable garden. Face to face
with stolid kokomuk in a seething wind,

into scale zooms the compost heap.
Up there, the sky's dark underbelly.
It was a fish. What is a fish now?

War jellies language – it was a fish
and then an eel that doubles back slippery,
changes register, shifts, disperses,

jostling, illusory. Tough wild parsnips.
Wire-worm in the spuds.
Cloudy, treacherous phrases muscling in.

Mute

It looked like craggy Alps
but it was a hillside pulverising.

I thought it was a food parcel
but it was a cluster bomb.

I thought it was a bullet hole
but it was a burn mark in the carpet.

The carpet is of wool, in a Persian pattern.
Transported on it to a war, we lie

among the rocks while parcels cluster,
smartly carpeting the mountains.

Ode to Wombat

In sleep your ruined lips droop,
your tongue sticks out like a petal.

Scarface, in your dream
your fangs are set in vice-grip jaws,

you're supple as a pup.
I call up memories of you

like holograms,
cathedrals of detail – here you are,

full tilt across the garden
to miss by a feather a black-backed gull

struggling to rise in the easterly;
climbing a hanging rope

with a snake-like contraction
of your neck muscles;

at Auahi, me drawing Rakiura,
black ink spattering on the bonnet,

you marking the territory.
When fate caught up with you

in a purple Honda,
you ground along the road for forty feet.

We keep your teeth in a small box,
what we could find of them,

in the ivory trail your jawbone drew
on Liffey Street.

Rakiura from Auahi

Omaui series

Frogs

The atmosphere is thinning –
the world is getting dirty

as the outer epidermis eats itself.
The frogs are vanishing.

Who will recall in Costa Rica
the webbed feet of the flying tree frog

filling like a parachute as it soars in the trees?
In Chile the four-eyed frog with eyes on its rump?

Gone without trace that drab frog
that flashes repellent patterns,

the Madagascan frog that turns bright red
and puffs up like a tomato?

Gone the ivory frog of the arum lily
that turns brown to match the dying blossoms?

Silent forever!
Who will remember

the bong-bong banjo
call of the pobblebonk?

Tourists (ii)

The pilgrims arrive at the Bluff signpost.
They come to the end quite suddenly
and peer out from the edge of the land
as if they might fall off into the sky.

They glimpse great breadth and distance,
a 'creamy reflection of ice'.
They call to windward inaudibly,
pointing to the signpost, to elsewhere.

They adopt funny poses for the camera.
Some of them run down the slope
and swing on the swing
at the end of the land, at the end of the world.

Immigration, 1810

Honekai's immigration policy
is unequivocal – on Rakiura

the sealing party from the *Sydney Cove*
patu-split in a flash,

all but fair young James Caddell,
sprawled in the shallows.

A certain princess loves blue eyes –
she keeps him, marries him.

Her uncle seeks knowledge
of those lands overseas

where (he has heard, disbelieving)
'the white man outnumbers the shells on the beach.'

Rakiura, 1823

At Poti Repo, Ebenezer Denton
died defending the stores –

the last thing he saw
was the patu

that struck like a shark
in the dreamy dark

where silent figures
cast and puffed

white flour about, bit soap
and spat it out,

scattered tobacco,
spurning the gunpowder,

throwing it down
on the ground, on the fire,

gyrating
through violent explosions.

Tuturau

At Tuturau, a monument
overlooks the Mataura:

'Here in 1836 the last fight took place
between North and South Island Maori,
when Chief Te Puoho led a war party
down the West Coast, over the Haast Pass
to Wanaka and over the Crown Range,
capturing the kaika at Tuturau.'

Tuhawaiki heard of it –
the waka came from Ruapuke
and Puoho died at dawn.

His head was stuck on a tall pole
facing whence he had come.

It's said that this was foretold at Ruapuke –
in the season of new potatoes,
a seer lay down to sleep on a woven sail
and dreamed of the seal-killer's eye –

Rowbulla's vanguard
advancing southwards,
stopped by a shot at Tuturau.

Millennial

Heading east to Ruapuke, look back sou'west
at rata staining black-green Motupohue.
To starboard 'the swirling whirlpools
of Tu Te Mataueka'. Beside your easy dance
my knuckles whiten on the rail.

In Henrietta's arc, from the dinghy
we walk up to the graveyard on the cape.
Boulders, windswept macrocarpa, clay.
Rain veils, unveils the gravestone.
Choked voice of a great-grandson
determined to finish his speech.

Hangi baskets on trestle tables under the trees.
Laughter, old names, stories born
of the house on the rocky hill.
I find you on the hillside
remembering your childhood,
gazing at misty Papatea.

In the kitchen, rain raps the roof. Suspended
above the hands of children, a rigged craft,
her hull devised from a swan's breastbone.
Now you reach up – touch the little boat.

Mosses, grasses, flax.
We lean against granite out of the wind
above the freshwater lagoon,
looking at Henrietta.

Here mice are called henriettas,
after the tiny immigrants from the *Elizabeth Henrietta,*
wrecked in 1824 in the bay
where the rocks called Puakihau's hair
jut like dreadlocks in rising wind.

In 1844 Bishop Selwyn saw: 'A beautiful evening:
Stewart's island hidden in mist.
Enormous blocks of granite in the centre,
the tops red with lichen; on the point to the left
a pillar of granite standing out against the sky –
on the right a pretty wooded bank
overhanging a small freshwater lake.
Large blocks of granite crowning the tops
of all the rising grounds.'

When Boultbee landed here in 1827
his boat was scuttled.
He was allowed to keep his Bible.
He found them clever, energetic, ruthless –
Tarbuka, Tuhawaiki –
names to conjure the mana of Ruapuke.

'One expects a savage', he wrote,
'accustomed to scenes of blood, to carry in his face
the looks indicative of a career of slaughter
& every murderous crime. Not so Tarbuka –
he was the most complete model of strength,
activity and elegance I had seen combined in any man.'

Dark cloaks the stones.
Two fishing boats, a granite pillar,
sunset red as the lichen on Pukepara.
A branch, furred with lichen – past our feet
a weka pecking, brown as a penny,
prospecting. Which way
next,
O cautious,
thorough,
perspicacious
Weka?

(Ruapuke, 1.1.2001)

Tracks

Green dawn,
black rock, lean cows.
Rakiura's taut skyline sings.

At certain places on this coast,
the past is as close
as the tilt of a pane –

they hold a record of events
as lodestones hold
the power of lightning.

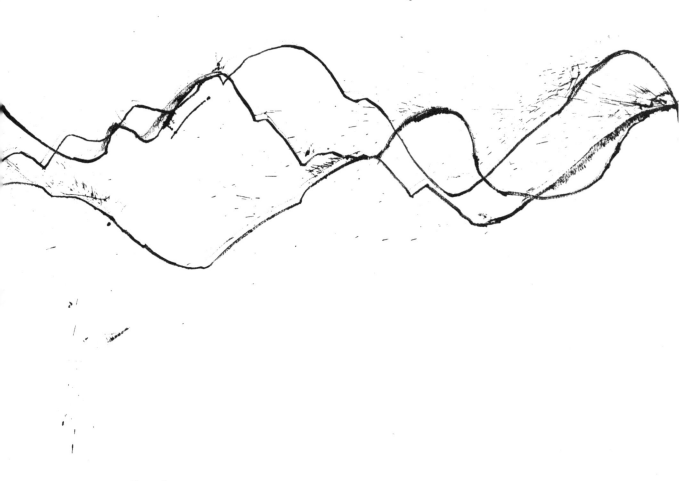

Omaui

Castle Rock

Lament

I came between you
and the world;

I was just your size;
we were pod and pea;

I took the brunt –
you wore me out.

Now I am had it,
quoth my boot.

Waiting

(for Jack Raukura)

At the doorway,
watch
a drip's
elastic
skin
contain

a slowly swelling
hanging world

until the dancing surface
stretches,

snaps
and spills
a drop.

With tiny speed
it starts again.

A flight of racing pigeons
in close-knit, subtly adjusting formation
swoops across the valley upside down.

Mist on Motupohue

Mist hangs in the valley.
The houses grow around the hill
above the sleepless port.

Weatherbeaten cottages
tidy as fishing boats
hold Bluff's warm heart.

Pohuehue weaves a cradle
with roots in the past,
which is dust;

rich compost for tendrils
enlacing, embracing
the family. Mist

sifts through the cabbage trees.
The world reverses in a raindrop,
balancing on a leaf like mercury.

Piano

Miss McKenzie used to guide
her pupils' fingers with a little stick.

In her piano's walnut knurls and knots,
sunlight discovers music.

Alone at night perhaps she played Mozart,
who twinkles in the stars without uncertainty,

while minuscule dimensions
furl beyond our ken,

or Chopin – when Bluff is still,
the flax frogs singing on the corner by the church,

I think I've heard arpeggios
rippling past the tips of willows.

Draughty

At dawn smoke lies like memory
above the houses.

Last night a tentacle of winter
brushed my side –

I was reminded
that the house is full of cracks.

Soundings – the wind testing gently,
teasing out melody –

our house
holds
true as a flute.

Complex

Reflections of sunset glittering
on that triumphant smelter complex
piss me off. It's sucking up
the power of southern lakes,
twinkling brashly where there should be only
beach and sky. Pale blue
deepens to pink at the horizon,
storm indigo coming in from the west.
A long swathe of nimbus sweeps above.
And then there's that tall chimney,
sticking up out of the landscape
like a flagrant cigarette.

Drawing

At the top of Motupohue, clematis island,
draw the coastline spread out full circle:

curving nor'east towards Tautuku,
westwards past Te Waewae,

south to the pathway chewed by Kewa
between here and Rakiura,

the crumbs that dropped
as islands from his mouth.

Spray from the strait
blows across Auahi like smoke.

Time slips a gear. The land reverts
to undisturbed tussock, flax, toetoe, fern.

In marks on paper I draw Auahi
out of this time and back in another,

or forward in another,
when all trace of us is gone.

Artist, 1773

William Hodges, Dusky Sound

She turned away, so close
he could have touched her.

He drew apart to map her jawline,
cheek, neck, feathers in her hair,

the spear she leaned on,
child slung on her back.

With his whittled, patient line
he drew her in and caught her.

Return

Kowhai, totara, iron lace
screen the old white house.
I walk around the verandah and feel eyes –
a possum glares from a trap.

The place is startlingly empty.
Jasmine pours over the fence
and up the lacebark.
Slow roots crack the asphalt path.

Somebody's looped a circlet of barbed wire
on a nail on the outside wall.
Warm smell of paint, turps,
caught between pages like a petal.

Between that departure, this return,
a slipping away – sense from memory
as the river from its silt – lees
in a salt-glazed crater fused to glass.

Knots

The sun has gone, the marigolds are closed.
The southerly whips the smile off the water,
raking the cabbage trees,
slim leaves blown like hair from a skull.

Hail batters the pane. I write by the coal range
while you knot Turk's Heads, telling me
about rounding South Cape on the *Mystery*
with the rags up in a howling gale
and running with the big roll coming home.

When you talk of birding on the manu
I hear them singing underground;
the soles of my feet remember
the cliff path's slope and camber
shaking me out like a bolt of tweed,
in gannet shoes along the brow of Conachair.

Your hands know knots by heart –
an open string, a journey;
a closed string, a return.
In strings, all possible worlds.

Wind beams through the floor.
To etch the gist of us two here against the dusk
would be delicate as Dürer –
the written threads cat's cradle in my fingers,
in yours the timeless patterns interweaving.

Awarua

Red

At tide's cusp falls the calm.
It seems the garden's never felt a storm.
Birdsong shimmers, a blowfly –
past and away, red-shifting.

Under sultry cloud cover, rain in the sun.
Two crimson blooms on a prickly stem;
the volunteer fire engine comes down the street;
the next red peeps from the wild fuchsia.

Warp

I couldn't hear myself think when the storm came over
and the roof became a giant drum.
Thunder rocked the house. Capricious lightning
reached a finger into my computer, knocked out the modem
and set the date back to 1956.

With a high tension flash, coming round the corner
the poles come off the wires and the trolleybus
stops in City Road like a questing insect.
The driver jumps out to relocate the pulley,
the boys stare out the back window.

Penny down the hill and tuppence up, in 1956
I'm clear as the mark of a sharp-to-cracking-point
Black Beauty on a clean page.
Cotton socks and schoolbag, with my new glasses
I can see every leaf on the tree.

Were I to live my life again, I'd have to live it just the same
anyhow, to be here and now abandoning the keyboard,
turning the whole show off for fear of electrocution
and going to the kitchen to make battered oysters
in a thunderstorm, retrieving my train of thought –

pull just one string and the whole caboodle unravels.

On the Roof

At dusk a rainbow stretched right over Dunedin.
We took our gins up to the roof.
Stone spires, rowan berries, autumn amber.
They met during the War.

He said once, 'You might see your life as a boat –
your birth splits the water, you move aft over time.'
Wind hushes the tall sequoia.
The Town Hall clock chimes the hour.

'At the stern, your life closes.'
City lights stripe the still harbour,
the sea black, sky black.
A leaf borne on the water,

resonances ripple from your encounters.
Ashes spiral in your wake.
Dad's eyes in the photo, Mum's solitary age –
the old ones keep their courage to the last.

Via Media

Deep in the brain between right and left
the electromagnetic charge around the corpus callosum
aligns nerve impulses, allowing them to flow
from one hemisphere to the other.

The motto of my grandmother
was 'Per via media tutissima.'

When she died she was as small as a bird,
but I remember her taller.
Indeed she was a wise interface,
the signal box of her family.

This bundle of nerves is at about ear-level.
I wiggle my ears, locating the via media,
imagining the centre where the impulses align,
a grandmother at the interface wisely regulating.

Daily life flows through her fingers
and passes into dream.
Dream washes out into the daylight
and disappears like foam.

Hauroko

An Apparition

Vice-Admiral Sir Richard Greynvile
walks into my study,
some details vague
but otherwise immaculate.

Please sit down, I say
to my hawkish genetic figment,
You have a lot to answer for.

A withering look assures me he prefers to stand
as if on the bridge of the *Revenge*,
staring over my head at Terra Nullius.

As I plunge into Ireland,
the creases at the corner of his mouth
deepen slightly.

At the plunder of America he rubs his jaw.
Mention of Indians stiffens his upper lip.

What else? Colonialism? The slave trade?
Heavy with his deeds and their reverberations
I roll a cigarette.

A pungent wisp tickles his nose. He sneezes.
His voice is like ground glass – Tobacco!

An Ignis Fatuus that bewitches
and leads Men into Pools and Ditches!

Recollection

Tobacco smoke
in velvet curtains –

Mary St Léger,
light as a feather –
she bore me sons.

On my return from sea
I find them
handsome and obedient,

my pellucid
wife
respectfully
hushing,
small waves lapping –

in the stifling comfort
of our gracious home

I hear the ocean calling.

Questions

Did you discern, Greynvile, I hazard,
when you claimed Roanoke
on behalf of the Virgin Queen,
the features
of Chief Wingina?

Or were they blurred
by the coppery gleam
of fabulous Chaunis Temoatan?

I thought I saw him wink.

Terra Nullius, he said at last,
scanning the horizon.
Finders, keepers.

How else finance our programmes
of imperial expansion in Virginia
equivalent to putting men on the moon?

Authority

Patrician wraith,
I'd like to introduce you to my husband.

If you had come to claim this land instead,
his archaic people might have been as docile
as the Croatoan Indians were at first –

I think more likely they'd have eaten you
and stuck your head on a tall post
facing the direction whence you came.

Greynvile seems put out and glances at me loftily.
My authority was plain, he rasps,
The flag was planted.

The Indians dug crops and made fish traps
while we built houses and a fort on English land.

My discipline was iron.
For theft of moonbeams in a silver cup
I razed the Indian village, Aquascogoc.

Insubstantial as the cobwebs on the window
he is fading with the light.

I ask again,
Did you see the features of those Indians,
or were they always slipping out of vision,
mere copper gleams among the leaves?

A Warning

Sir Richard in shirtsleeves
wandering in the forest.
Lost, lost, he mutters angrily,
lost colony!

I left them with Lane
and sailed home for supplies,
to be back by Easter, 1586,
but the Spanish war delayed me –
when I came back in the autumn
they were gone.

Mineral-hungry,
in the lean season
they had begun to starve.

Wingina was killed;
the tribes were angry.
Drake had come past and picked them up.

I left fifteen men to guard the empty fort
and set to sea again.

It was a warning.

When John White came in 1587,
with a replacement expedition,
he found but one white man on Roanoke,
a skeleton.

Lost Colony

Greynvile, did you hear what happened then
to the colony that you began?
The fort was desolate, the season late
for sailing on to Chesapeake Bay,
so with prickling hair on the back of their necks
they set to repairing the thatchless houses
laced with melon vines, 'and Deere within them,
feeding on those Melons.'

One of the colonists was killed by the Indians
down by the creek.
Governor White killed friendly Croatoans
in error, at Dasamonquepeuc.
He had the English-speaking Indian, Manteo,
christened and declared him Lord of Roanoke –
but supplies again ran low.

White must himself set off for England
to petition in person for support,
leaving behind the colonists,
including his granddaughter Virginia,
first English newborn in America.

But war raged on the Spanish Main.
White returned at last in 1590,
having lost a boat and crew, chasing Indian smoke,
and spent the night at anchor just off Roanoke
playing English tunes on a trumpet
to give the colony good cheer.

In the morning when he went ashore
he found the settlement empty;
no clue to the fate of the colonists
but scattered papers among melon vines,
and CROATOAN carved on a tree.

Revenge

Do the dead see it all as a whole, Sir Richard?
What drove you head first into the Armada?
Tennyson claims that after the solemn Spanish
bore you defeated to their flagship
and laid you by the mast,
you rose heroically to speak
of Queen and Faith, then fell down dead.

Others have the Spanish captains
proposing toasts to the English warrior
who had fought them fifteen hours –
you quaffed their wine and crunched their crystal goblets
in your teeth and swallowed them.
Dying took three days.
The *Revenge* went down without you.

The Glory Track

Lakiula sings across the strait
between blue and blue.

The landscape takes the electric reins
that drive my hand.

Like a voice, a ghost ship comes to me
across the water, a chimerical

encryption that appears and disappears
in passage through the dreaming ocean.

In Dusky Sound, the *Resolution*
seemed to the watchers a floating island;

the *Endeavour* as she ghosted past,
sounding the coast, a wraith.

It is said, Sir Walter Ralegh's ship
appeared 'in gallant posture'

among the early settlers of Carolina;
colonial wrack strews Greynvile's wake.

There's the *Priscilla*, with thirty-six St Kildans
bound for Australia in 1853,

never to return to their antlered island,
where, defying the minister, the poet

Euphemia McCrimmon sang aloud
the ancient pagan songs, lest they be lost.

'Thou gavest me the first honied fulmar'
reminds me of Stu preparing roasted, fresh titi,

shining with oil and stuffed with peaches.
We're very partial to them.

The St Kildans were very partial to tobacco.
If you ran out you had to 'chew your waistcoat pocket

and wait patiently till spring'.
Finlay MacQueen must have thought he'd seen a ghost

in 1918, when, tilling the crofts, chewing,
he saw a German submarine

surface in Village Bay like a sea monster.
Undeterred by the First World War,

he rowed out to enquire whether the sailors
of this strange craft had any tobacco,

as he was severely depleted.
When seventy-two shells peppered the shore,

he rowed back with alacrity.
Now I see clinker-built *If*, X-class,

with us children learning to sail her
under Dad's curt instruction. I never quite got the hang

of the centreboard. His voice intoning 'The Ballad
of the *Revenge*' plays on my mind like flame.

There are many ghost ships on this coast,
wrecked in the straits and at the entrance to the harbour

where wind shears the vegetation to the hill
and seas crash green below the Glory Track.

When *England's Glory* with her shifting cargo
came to grief here in 1881, the survivors

staggered along to the Bluff, Glory be,
and the track was trodden deep by salvagers.

If the sea's deep dance
is memory, its surface is the present –

across the moment falls a blur of spray, a feather.
Ghost ships under weigh glide through my dreams.

Meanwhile

Meanwhile, apart,

as steam curls
from the earth,

my soundings
round
on my own

heart-springs,

that stubborn,
makeshift

energy, deep
as the cirrus in heaven,

fired by some fleck
of fusion

that I carry
from the sun.

From love and grief,
all I have learned

is Time.